MW00442977

This Journal
Belongs To: